D1010832

ILLITERACY

TROUBLED

SOCIETY

ILLITERACY

Elizabeth Sirimarco

The Rourke Corporation, Inc.
Vero Beach, Florida 32964

To my father,
Thank you

Human history becomes more and more a race
between education and catastrophe.
-H.G. Wells

The Rourke Corporation, Inc.
P.O. Box 3328, Vero Beach, FL 32964

Grateful acknowledgement is made to Houghton Mifflin Co. for permission to reprint material from *Read With Me,* copyright 1990 by Walter Anderson.
Special thanks to the Literacy Volunteers of America for providing photographs.

Sirimarco, Elizabeth.
   Illiteracy / by Elizabeth Sirimarco.
     p. cm. — (Troubled society)
   Includes index.
   Summary: Discusses illiteracy and the problems it causes, as well as ways of eliminating it in our society.
     ISBN 0-86593-115-1
     1. Literacy—United States—Juvenile literature. 2. Literacy—Social aspects—United States—Juvenile literature.
   [1. Literacy.] I. Title. II. Series.
   LC151.S57   1991
   302.2'244'0937—dc20   91-7168
                                                CIP
                                                  AC

Series Editor: Gregory Lee
Editor: Marguerite Aronowitz
Book design and production: The Creative Spark,
   Capistrano Beach, CA
Cover photograph: Joseph Nettis/Photo Researchers, Inc.

ILLITERACY

Contents

ONE

THE PROBLEM IS GROWING

Hårmoden skifter, men dit hår
er det samme. Det skal holde
til meget; vejr og vind, hårbørste
og føntørrer, permanenter og farvninger.

Chances are good that you cannot read or understand the words above. Your teachers and parents don't expect you to know the Danish language, even the simple advertising copy shown here. But if those same words were translated into English, and you still could not read them, you would be among the approximately 27 million Americans to whom written English is as foreign as Danish, Russian, or Chinese.

Imagine for a minute that you never learned to read. When you were younger, it wasn't much of a problem. When a teacher asked you to read out loud, you could lie and say you lost your glasses on the way to school. Or you had a sore throat. Or you forgot your book. You knew a hundred different excuses. Your teacher would become a little concerned. Maybe she kept you after class or tried to meet with your parents. But there were a lot of kids in your class, and eventually that teacher gave up and let you move on to the next grade.

In junior high, it was a little more difficult to fool the teachers. You cheated to pass tests. Sometimes you paid a friend to write papers for you. Your grades were barely passing, and you couldn't wait until you were old enough to drop out of school. You were sure it

Too many United States citizens leave elementary school
without ever learning to read.

would be easier for you in the real world.

Finally, at 16 or 17, you leave school. Suddenly
you realize how hard it is to get a job when you're *illiterate*. As an illiterate, you have little or no reading and
writing skills. You can't read the want ads in the newspaper. You can't fill out an application form. When you
finally find a job pumping gas, your boss says he
doesn't mind that you can't read. You think it's because
he can pay you a lot less than the employees who han-
dle money or fix cars.

You walk three miles to and from work each
day. You won't take the bus because you can't tell if
you're on the right one, and you're too embarrassed to

ask the driver. You'd like to get your driver's license—maybe even buy a used car—but you can't study the manual or take the written test. Sometimes friends ask you to meet them at a movie theater or a restaurant where you've never been. You can't read the street signs to follow directions, so you stay home. And it doesn't work to ask people for help. They think you know how to read like everyone else, so their directions are useless.

Every day you run into a new problem. You go to the doctor or dentist, and the forms the receptionist asks you to fill out are impossible to read. You try to get a bank account, and there are still more papers to read and sign. You're trying so hard to keep your illiteracy a secret, so you can't ask for help. All of a sudden, you realize it isn't any easier to be illiterate once you're out of school. In fact, it's more difficult.

How Many Illiterate Americans?

Fortunately, you can read. These problems may never be part of your life. But there are about 250 million people in the United States, and at least ten percent of them are illiterate. Looked at another way, there are 193 million people over the age of 14 in our country. If 27 million of these individuals cannot read, then nearly 15 percent of our adult population is illiterate. One expert estimates that the United States ranks 49th among the 158 nations in the United Nations in literacy level. Even if you have excellent reading skills, even if you've never met a person who is illiterate, the problem still affects you and your family because you live here. It doesn't only affect the poor. And it doesn't only happen to "stupid" people.

The Power Of Language

What is all knowledge but recorded history?
-Thomas Carlyle

Benjamin Lee Whorf, a *linguist* (someone who studies languages), described language as a complex system. This system allows us to do three things: communicate with others, think, and acquire knowledge that helps us form opinions and beliefs about our world. While spoken communication is important, the recording of information and experience has the ability to outlast human life. That means the written word has the power to preserve history more accurately than the spoken word. As the old saying goes, one who does not know history is doomed to repeat it. Written communication has helped us to understand our civilization's history. It has helped us learn from mistakes made by our ancestors. With it we pass on important inventions and ideas to new generations. Although written words can still be incorrect, or filled with the ideas and prejudices of the author, they can last and be judged.

Perhaps you've played a game called Whisper in one of your classes. Let's say the first player whispers this sentence in someone's ear: "I read the magazine *Newsweek*." The same thing is whispered from player to player. When the last person has heard the sentence, she repeats aloud what she has heard: "I saw the news last week." Very often the sentence has

Reading a car repair manual is just one of the many
tasks that literate people take for granted.

been changed from its original form because each person might say it just a little bit differently. When a number of speakers tell the same story over a period of time, it is likely that the story will lose its accuracy. Once a story has been written down, however, it can remain in its original form as long as the text survives.

How Did Written Language Develop?

While no one knows exactly when written language first developed, many archaeologists believe that the first attempts to preserve information were in *pictographs*. Pictographs are drawings that represent something. A young cave dweller who went hunting for the first time might have drawn a large animal on the wall of his cave to remember the event. If two or more pictographs are combined to make the meaning more clear, it becomes an *ideograph*. Perhaps the cave dweller would have drawn a human-like figure holding a spear to communicate more clearly the idea of the hunt.

The next step toward language was to create specific symbols or signs to represent spoken words, or *logographs*. Many early civilizations established their own logographic systems, including the Chinese and the Mayans. Have you learned about the ancient Egyptians' *hieroglyphics*? These early forms of writing were more precise than pictographs and ideographs, but there were so many symbols to represent different objects that literacy was limited to only a few scholars. Also, abstract thoughts like happiness or love were hard to communicate through pictures.

Finally, in the eighth and ninth centuries BC

(eight or nine hundred years before Christ), the Greek alphabet was developed. This was a much smaller number of symbols (only 24 characters) that represented the sounds of the Greek language. With the help of a democratic government, the first truly literate culture was born. Many texts were written at this time that are still read today, including the work of the Greek philosopher Plato and the epic poems of Homer, *The Iliad* and *The Odyssey*. Finally, the Latin alphabet evolved from the Greek one—and we still use it today.

Is Illiteracy A New Problem?

Throughout history, there have been periods when literacy seemed unnecessary for survival. Ancient Rome learned to appreciate the written word from the Greeks, but when they were conquered by the illiterate Germans in the fifth century AD (*anno Domini* or after Christ), literacy was lost.

In the period known as The Dark Ages, from the late fifth century until approximately 1000 AD, only about one or two percent of Europe was literate. While the written word remained important in India and China, the Catholic Church was the only home of European literacy. Monks copied and studied religious texts, but very little original work was written or read.

After the year 1000, literacy slowly began to gain importance. At first only the upper classes were literate, but eventually political and religious leaders found they could persuade people with the written word. Reading and writing became powerful tools for teaching ideas. People were taught to read and respect standard materials, like the Bible, and literacy became a way of achieving a more moral society, or a more stable government. Sometimes it became a way to convey revolutionary ideas and cause change. Often it became a way for church and state to control the people by controlling what they read.

When the world became industrialized in the 19th century, it was necessary for even more people to read and write. Women, who had long been deprived of education, were finally acquiring reading and writing skills. By the end of the century, more than half of the European population was literate.

Literacy Today

In the 20th century, the goal of a completely literate population has touched nearly every country around the world. Many people see it as a way of *empowering*, or giving power, independence, and self-reliance to the individual. This goal inspired the United Nations to call 1990 "The Year of International Literacy." It prompted President George Bush to make July 2, 1990, the first National Literacy Day. It caused 30 percent of companies in the United States to offer remedial education courses to their employees.

The quest for literacy has led countries from the Soviet Union to Tanzania, and Germany to Nicaragua to establish programs that offer to help illiterate citizens learn to read. Each year more adult non-readers across the United States muster the courage it takes to learn to read, and new volunteers offer their time and knowledge to teach them.

Many see literacy as a means of fighting

social problems like crime, unemployment, drug abuse, a failing national economy, and racism. About 50 percent of people on welfare are illiterate, probably because it is difficult for non-readers to find jobs to support themselves. Also, 50 percent of the United States prison population is illiterate, which suggests that illiteracy plays a role in a person's decision to turn to crime.

Nearly 45 percent of African-American adults are *functionally illiterate*, or unable to read above a third- or fourth-grade level. And though Hispanic adults in the United States are often literate in their mother tongue, 56 percent of them are illiterate in English. High levels of illiteracy among minorities help to keep prejudice and negative stereotypes alive in the United States.

If illiteracy makes people unemployable, it will affect an entire country. If illiteracy forces a person to commit a crime to survive, it will affect us all. Literacy empowers. It gives people the power to support themselves, to take part in government, and to acquire knowledge. The literate person can be self-reliant. The literate person can make decisions, vote, and take part in a democratic government. The literate person can have a satisfying career.

Of course illiteracy is not the cause of all our country's problems, and illiterates are not bad or inferior people. A higher level of literacy will not eliminate all social problems. But literacy *can* affect national productivity, the crime rate, and racism. As First Lady Barbara Bush has said, "If we can lick the problem of people being functionally illiterate...we will then go on to solve most of the other major problems besetting this country." Perhaps this is too great a task to accomplish with a single solution, but achieving 100 percent literacy is a good place to start.

TWO

HOW DO PEOPLE BECOME ILLITERATE?

Every illiterate person has their own story; there is no one reason why a person reaches adulthood without learning to read. For some, there may have been special circumstances at home that made it difficult to study or concentrate in class. Maybe a student was abused by a troubled parent, or moved from town to town so often that he or she couldn't keep up with other classmates. Some students may have a more difficult time learning than others. And sometimes the school system isn't working as well as it should.

Learning In America

People as different as rock singer Janet Jackson and author H.G. Wells have spoken out about the inadequate education system in the United States. Politicians and citizens around the country have begun to question the effectiveness of public education in America. Yet in the 1980s, the Reagan Administration continued efforts to cut federal education programs. Reagan's Secretary of Education, William Bennett, toured the country to speak about the importance of education, yet supported presidential budget cuts that ignored the decline in the quality of American public schooling.

If public education were working, then 10 percent of our population would not be functionally illiterate. What's going wrong in the United States public school system today? This is not an easy question to answer, and many people have different opinions about the problems and potential solutions.

A teacher can make a lot of difference in the way a student learns.
Many teachers believe that each student needs personal attention
to succeed to their fullest potential.

One report on education in America recently said of the typical classroom, "The emotional tone is neither harsh and punitive nor warm and joyful; it might accurately be described as flat." Think about the classes you've enjoyed in school. What was it that made them special? Probably not memorizing dates from the American Revolution or multiplication tables. The classes we seem to enjoy are the ones where learning changes us in some way, when we become excited by what we discover. Maybe the class focused on a special interest, like a biology class that studies animals. Perhaps the course took special field trips to a zoo or a veterinary office. Maybe the class was taught by a teacher who brought excitement to even the most boring subject.

There is no way to inspire an entire class of students. And a teacher can't be expected to be enthusiastic every day of the year. But for a classroom to be a successful one, the students must want to learn and the teacher must want to teach. Percy Fleming is a man in his late twenties who studies in an adult literacy program. When asked why he never learned to read as a child, he replied, "I'm sure I was a slow learner, but I realize today, looking back, that the answer to that question also has something to do with the way we define the word *teacher.* We had several of those in my elementary school. They would show up every day and stand in the front of the classroom and they'd talk.... They would hand out papers, and they'd pick up papers. They'd do the same thing every hour, every day, every year. I guess they did just about everything a teacher is supposed to do except teach.

"I was one of at least four students—and there were probably more—who could not read in the third grade. But we were passed anyway, maybe because we weren't troublesome, or maybe only because no one noticed."

Fewer and fewer people are choosing teaching as a career because the salaries and recognition are low, although many experts believe this will change in the future. Of those who do become teachers, the best choose the schools with the highest budgets and middle- to upper-class students. Schools in poor neighborhoods have special problems. Why would teachers want the extra challenge, even the danger, of teaching in a poor neighborhood when plenty of "good" neighborhoods need teachers, too?

The United States government has chosen to make education a priority only after other needs are met. Our leaders express concern that countries such as Japan and Germany have more productive economies—economies that are in part the product of better school systems and a higher percentage of educated citizens. American leaders worry about our country's increasingly poor performance in academics, yet refuse to challenge our current education system. They continue to place little value on teachers.

An important step in destroying adult illiteracy is to take a long, hard look at early prevention of this problem in our elementary and high schools. Along with the steps taken to help illiterate adults, a successful fight against illiteracy will see to it that the nation's young people do not leave the school system without knowing how to read. Our population must not only *attend* school, but *learn* there as well.

Now that Percy Fleming has learned to read, he knows how important it is. What has it given him? "Power," he says. "Power to say '*I know*.' I can find out information, I can get knowledge myself. By reading, I've learned about other people—and that has given me insight, helped me to grow, even given me courage. Now I even dream about reading and writing." What Percy has described is what education should accomplish in everyone.

Health Problems

Anna, a bright mother of three, has a beautiful home. Her children are well-behaved, intelligent, and friendly. Anna is an excellent mother and wife. No one would believe she never learned to read.

When Anna was growing up, she had a health problem that sent her to the hospital two or three times a year, sometimes for over a month at a time. When she first began learning the alphabet, she became sick and was out of school for two months. When she finally felt well enough to return to school, her classmates could already put letters together to make words. Her teachers tried to help her catch up, but there just wasn't enough time in the day. They wanted the sickly Anna to feel like a normal, healthy child, so they never gave her special work or suggested summer school.

By the time Anna was in high school, her health had improved. Unfortunately, her academic skills had not. She barely scraped by, taking as many gym, art, home economics, and simple math classes as she could. Somehow, Anna graduated from high school without being able to read better than a second or third grader.

Excessive absence from school, for illness or any other reason, can make learning a significant challenge for a child. Sometimes a parent will try to coach the student through lessons; sometimes special classwork can be sent home. Even so, valuable class time is lost. Once a student is behind, it can be impossible to catch up. And a student may never read as well as society demands.

Poverty

We like to think of our country as a powerful, strong nation, one that offers all of its citizens equal rights. We want to believe that all people in the United States have equal opportunity. We do not want to believe that anyone is less likely to be successful simply because of skin color, sex, or social class. Literacy is very often a reflection of social and economic conditions. And the poorer a person is or the worse the neighborhood a person lives in, the more likely it is that he or she may never learn to read.

Linwood Earl Johnson was in his mid-thirties when he began taking literacy classes at the Metro Volunteer Literacy Program of Nashville, Tennessee. Within a year, he could read at the fifth-grade level and has progressed steadily forward since then.

When Linwood was growing up in the 1960s, his family didn't have much money, but they worked hard to support themselves. Each year he would miss four or five months of school to help pick and chop cotton in the fields. His family lived in rural Mississippi. Linwood's teachers knew where he and some of his classmates were when they were absent from school. They also understood that the missed classes were a matter of survival for their families, and did not interfere. But Linwood missed just enough school to make reading difficult for him. As time went by, Linwood grew frustrated. He was tired of pretending he could read, and dropped out before he graduated from high school.

After years of low paying jobs, Linwood finally decided it was time to learn to read. After two years of tutoring, he was able to read books, newspapers, and almost anything else he could get his hands on, including *The Helen Keller Story*.

"That touched me," says Linwood. "Here was this lady who was blind and deaf, but she returned to school to learn to read and write....Now, I thought, if this woman who was blind and deaf could learn, then I, who can see and hear, can learn."

Linwood is an excellent example of a successful adult literacy program. His progress is so exceptional that he has been the honored guest of President and Mrs. Bush, and he has been featured on a national TV commercial about illiteracy.

Reading Disabilities

Some people who never learn to read have special problems that make it difficult for them to learn. *Reading disabilities* are biological problems that slow or completely prevent a student from learning. For example, sometimes the brain has a difficult time decoding the symbols that make up the alphabet. Some students may learn to cope with their handicap on their own, although the result is usually poor performance. Some become troublemakers in class to draw attention away from their schoolwork. Others try to behave perfectly and hope that teachers won't notice them. A concerned teacher or another person at school may recognize a particular student's difficulty in class. Unfortunately, however, reading disabilities often go undetected or are mistaken for limited intelligence.

Perhaps the most frustrating of learning disabilities, one which can often result in illiteracy, is *dyslexia*. Dyslexia is an actual difficulty or inability to read, spell, or write words.

A man named Charles L. Shedd conducted important studies on dyslexia. He recognized a number of symptoms common to the disability, such as confusing letters like *b* and *d* or *p* and *q*, or reversing the order of numbers (*49* instead of *94*). A dyslexic child can also suffer from poor coordination or clumsiness; stuttering; difficulty in knowing left from right; short attention span; hyperactivity; and low self-esteem. There are many other characteristics found in the dyslexic child. A person who has one or two of these symptoms does not necessarily suffer from the disability. A professional often has difficulty diagnosing dyslexia, but if it is recognized before a child is in third grade, chances are good that they can be helped with special education.

Children with dyslexia are often misunderstood. Their teachers might think they are stupid or "acting up." They may be told their talents lie in sports or art, or even math and science, but that reading "just isn't your thing."

Sally Osbourne (not her real name), a teacher and graduate of Harvard University, remembers a seventh grade teacher who asked her to stand up and read. "I couldn't recognize even one word on the page. After what seemed an eternity, the teacher got angry and told me to go into another classroom where I was to write, again and again, 'I am stupid because I cannot read.'" Unfortunately, the teacher did not recognize her problem and never tried to help her.

Sally wondered why most adults at her schools chose to ignore her. She struggled through

Albert Einstein had dyslexia, but it didn't keep him from
making one of the most important scientific discoveries of our time—
the Theory of Relativity.

school only with the help of her friends and mother, receiving poor but passing grades. And although she had never learned to read, Sally went on to a state college and eventually became a teacher.

"College was a struggle from the start," says Sally. She took only classes with oral tests, projects and papers because she was unable to take written exams. "Four years later, I earned a bachelor's degree—or perhaps I should say my mother and I earned one. She read many of the textbooks to me; she transcribed the ideas from my head onto paper; she pushed me to accept new challenges."

After college, Sally taught first and second graders. She had a teaching assistant who taught the students *phonics,* a method of teaching beginners to read using the sounds of the alphabet. If Sally was telling a story from a book and couldn't remember the rest, she would put the book down and ask the children to tell her what might happen next. She and her students went for long walks in the country, where Sally would demonstrate math and science in nature. The test scores of Sally's students were good. Her alternative teaching methods seemed to work, and her students enjoyed school.

One day Sally visited another teacher's class-room, a class for special-needs children. For the first time, Sally began to suspect that she had a reading disability. She applied to Harvard Graduate School and was accepted. It was there that Sally was finally diagnosed as dyslexic. The school offered special ser-vices, and she began to learn to read. With the help of understanding teachers, Sally received an advanced degree from Harvard, and now she is literate.

Dyslexia

The word *dyslexia*, like many English words, comes from the ancient Greek language. It means difficulty reading. But while reading is often the most difficult task for a dyslexic, it can make other activities, like dancing or telling a story, challenging. No one is certain what causes dyslexia, but scientists know it is a brain malfunction. It can be compared to a computer that has all the necessary parts, but something isn't connected quite right. It works differently than other computers.

The brain is made up of two hemispheres, or halves. One controls body movements, the other controls language. Many specialists believe that in the dyslexic's case, neither hemisphere has become stronger than the other. Confusion develops between the halves as the body performs routine tasks.

Some studies have concluded that as many as 10 percent of all people are dyslexic, but most can and have learned to overcome their learning difference. In fact, a number of dyslexics have gone on to become noted thinkers and writers, among them scientist Albert Einstein, British statesman Winston Churchill, inventor Thomas Edison, athlete Bruce Jenner, and artist-scientist-philosopher Leonardo da Vinci. There is no question that dyslexics can go on to succeed in any field.

The Reasons

People are functionally illiterate for a number of reasons. Maybe it's ineffective teachers. Or social problems like poverty and racism. It might be a reading disability like dyslexia. Regardless of the reasons, students are making it through school without learning to read. Or they are dropping out because they can't cope with the frustration of being unable to read. Having a literate nation means that we need to look hard at our education system.

We need to make changes. We need to make certain that all Americans have the opportunity to receive a good education: from the poorest people in the inner cities to rural farm children; from middle-class students in our suburbs to those who speak another language as their "mother tongue." We must recognize and help reading-disabled students. We need to concern ourselves with high-risk students in our schools today, the ones who are most apt to become illiterate adults. And as we teach them to read, we will be doing something about illiteracy.

THREE

WHY IS LITERACY IMPORTANT?

The media has given the problem of illiteracy a great deal of attention in recent years. The American Broadcasting Companies (ABC) runs commercials using its prime-time television stars to tell viewers how important reading is. Congressmen and women around the country are trying to pass legislation to fund literacy programs. Both the United Nations and the Pope have taken action to bring international illiteracy to the public's attention. Barbara Bush has made adult illiteracy her number one cause. And on July 29, 1990, President Bush issued a Presidential Proclamation about the importance of literacy and education in America:

If the United States is to remain a free, strong, and prosperous country and a force for good in the world, we must cultivate the talent and potential of all our people—in the work place, in our families and in our communities.

What makes literacy so important that leaders in the United States and around the world are concerned about it?

The Costs Of Illiteracy

Illiteracy *does* cause problems for society, although this can be difficult to prove. As we've noted, an illiterate person experiences low self-esteem and difficulty in finding a job. Illiterate employees risk injuries on the job because they are unable to read manuals describing proper use of dangerous equipment. Often the quality of products

The job hunt can be frustrating—even impossible—for an illiterate person.

is lessened and customers are dissatisfied when employees are unable to follow written instructions in the workplace. Corporations spend nearly $10 billion each year on reading, writing, and math classes for employees who need to catch up.

It is difficult to calculate the exact cost of illiteracy, but it clearly take its toll on our economy. According to former Secretary of Education T. H. Bell, it costs approximately $6 billion each year to keep illiterate prisoners, who make up half of all inmates, in jail. The large number of non-readers in prison indicates that there is a connection between illiteracy and crime, so a percentage of that $6 billion could be saved if there were fewer illiterate individuals.

Author Jonathan Kozol estimated that the direct costs of illiteracy add up to about $20 billion annually for prisons, welfare received by illiterate individuals, and industrial and military accidents. The indirect costs of illiteracy may be as high as $100 billion due to the decrease in our nation's gross national product and productivity. The American Library Association claims that functionally illiterate adults cost $224 billion annually in welfare payments, crime, job incompetence, lost taxes, and remedial education.

The Information Age

"American jobs are placing greater demands on employees," said a 1990 Senate Labor Committee report. "The average American worker today must have skills at the ninth-grade through 12th-grade levels, not the fourth-grade level typical after World War II. And the standards keep rising."

In coming years, the greatest number of new jobs will be those requiring the most education. We live in a time called the Information Age because of great technological advances that have occurred in the past 40 years. It is a time when many companies sell information instead of goods, which means ideas and solutions will be the products of the future. Computers and software are part of this revolution, as are medical technology and investment services.

As our world continues to grow increasingly complex, the number of jobs calling for unskilled labor is declining. Every year new inventions make our lives easier, more entertaining, safer, and longer. But our increasingly technical world has placed higher demands on people in the work force.

The Department of Education has estimated that 24 to 30 percent of unskilled and semi-skilled workers in the United States read below the fourth grade level.

The end of the 20th century will see a shortage of jobs for these workers, and not enough workers who have the education and training necessary to fill the high-tech jobs that will dominate the job market. David Kearns, chief executive officer of Xerox Corporation (one of the largest companies in the United States), has said that the basic skills of the nation's work force "are simply not good enough for the United States to compete in a world economy."

Many United States companies have found this to be the case. New York Telephone Company had to give an entry-level exam to 60,000 people to hire just 3,000 because 84 percent failed the test. Chemical Bank in New York interviews 40 applicants to find one who can successfully be trained as a teller. At Chrysler Corporation, a worker who detects a flaw is supposed to push a button that reads "bad hood fit." Unfortunately, many of Chrysler's employees couldn't read the instruction, so the company has begun to use pictures instead of words on its assembly-line equipment.

Illiteracy can also cause workplace accidents. It can decrease productivity. It can be blamed for customer dissatisfaction. And it can slow a company's growth because employees are not able to use new technology. Kearns, like many other employers, feels that the American education system has put our population at a disadvantage. He suggests that every student should be expected to complete college entrance requirements, whether or not they intend to continue their education or not, in order to compete with the superior education programs in other countries—particularly Japan. Unfortunately, 70 percent of the work force that will be in place in the year 2000 is already out of school. And it isn't enough to look only at our education system—we need both preventive medicine *and* a cure.

United States corporations have already begun programs to aid illiterate employees. As many as 75 percent of large U.S. corporations offer some type of education to raise employee literacy, including Polaroid, Planters Peanuts, and Simon and Schuster. Some companies work with outside community agencies or labor unions. Others have programs within their organizations. Although some corporations tightly screen potential employees for literacy, others, like Aetna Life and Casualty Co., offer training curriculum in basic business skills for both entry-level illiterate workers and current employees with educational problems.

Managers and supervisors try to recognize employees who have math or reading problems. They can encourage them to become involved in a company-sponsored program or refer them to a community service. The most successful education programs have often been job related, and therefore, the workplace is an excellent place to combat illiteracy.

The Business Council for Effective Literacy (BCEL) works to make the executives of major American companies aware of illiteracy. Dan Lacy, planner for the BCEL, explains why corporations are willing to spend so much money educating their employees: "Illiteracy is not a problem whose solution can be free of major costs, but we know the price of *not* dealing with the problem will be far greater than the price of attacking it meaningfully."

For Individual Or Country?

A 1989 study suggested that the goal of adult literacy programs should be to "ensure that by the year 2000 or soon thereafter, every adult has the skills needed to perform effectively the tasks required by a high-productivity economy...." While the effect of illiteracy on the economy is important, adult illiteracy experts continue to stress individual empowerment as the first goal of illiteracy campaigns.

One problem of focusing entirely on the economics of illiteracy is that it places the blame for our nation's economic problems on non- or low-literate adults. It forgets the power and liberation literacy offers the individual. Most individuals who enroll in adult literacy programs do so for education rather than for employment. When non-readers become readers, they will be able to use their knowledge for their own success as well as that of their country.

Frank C. Laubach, a pioneer in 20th century literacy efforts, once said, "Educated people are seldom hungry. The dividing line between hunger and plenty is identical with the line between illiteracy and education." The person who can read can take care of him or herself. They accomplish two goals: empowerment and competence.

Literacy And Our Government

One of the most important things about being a United States citizen is our right to vote. Having the right to choose our leaders and the laws that govern our lives is what our forefathers fought for. But having the right to vote is often meaningless to the illiterate or semi-literate person. A totally illiterate person cannot read the ballot to vote, much less register to vote.

Ted Carson, a California resident, can read at the fifth grade level—well enough to fill out simple forms, write checks, and function in his job as a dishwasher. Since Ted is able to read most of the words on the ballot, you might think he is able to make a decision when it comes time to vote. Unfortunately, understanding the meaning is a little more difficult than simply being able to read the words.

It takes more than a fifth grader's reading ability to vote. The wording on the ballot is not always clear, and neither are the actual results of the proposed legislation. For example, Ted wouldn't know that a certain proposition might end up costing the taxpayers $4 million if it wins. Although the county in which he lives sent all registered voters a detailed booklet explaining the advantages and disadvantages of each proposition, Ted couldn't understand what he was reading.

Ted could, however, hear radio and television ads that usually offer one-sided and confusing information. A commercial might feature his favorite television star talking about a proposition: "Don't vote for proposition 16," says the celebrity. "If it passes, more than a 100,000 trees will be cut down in a California forest next year."

Maybe what the commercial says is true. But the proposition may plan to have trees cut down in an *overgrown* forest, then use the wood to build homes for the poor. The commercial doesn't tell Ted the whole story. The commercial didn't lie, it simply oversimplified the proposition. So Ted chose to vote against the proposition because a celebrity told him a half-truth. If he were able to read and understand the proposition, as literate people are able to do, he might have voted *for* the proposition.

As we can see, Ted is unable to cast an informed vote, and is therefore deprived of his right to have a say in the United States government. Many literate citizens choose not to vote because the issues are too difficult to understand. The majority of illiterate citizens do not vote, and often those who do are poorly informed. This is one more situation where those who cannot read and understand are unable to help themselves.

Frank Laubach said, "You think it is a pity they cannot read, but the real tragedy is that they have no voice in public affairs, they never vote, they are never represented in any conference. They are the silent victims, the forgotten men..." Illiteracy can deprive a United States citizen of his or her rights. We cannot hope to be a democratic and just country when at least 27 million citizens are unable to voice their opinions about their government.

The publisher of the *Miami Herald* newspaper,

So many things that readers take for granted are significant challenges to those who cannot read. An illiterate person cannot compare prices or nutritional values at the grocery.

David Lawrence, Jr., describes the role of literacy in a democratic government this way: "The last two hundred years have taught us that this country works best when the rights, the intelligence, and the capacities of human beings are respected. *People have a right to know.* That wonderful notion, so forcefully recorded in the First Amendment, is the foundation of the business I'm in—that if we give enough information, enough comment, people can make up their own minds. For me, it's as basic as 'What do we want this country to be? How do we keep it free? How do we make it safe for the next generation?' I think we can answer wisely as a nation only when our fellow citizens are informed, and to me the ability to read is directly related to being an informed citizen."

"Inherited" Illiteracy

Illiteracy seems to form an endless circle: illiterate parents are far more likely to raise illiterate children. In fact, some studies have concluded that academic success is more closely related to a student's family background than to the school he or she attended. It makes sense that children from literate homes will learn more easily than those from illiterate backgrounds.

Very often, illiterate parents don't offer their children encouragement to learn. Illiteracy can be passed on to children both intentionally and unintentionally. For example a mother who is unable to read stories to her children before they start school cannot give her children a love for books and reading. Maybe she needs a lot of help around the house when her children get home from school, so they never have time to study. A father might feel threatened by a son or daughter who is learning things he never did, so he'll discourage their efforts. Illiterate parents are less likely to enforce strict homework rules and more apt to raise children who will one day drop out of school.

Although a student's home life can greatly influence his or her performance in school, one educator feels that a discouraging family can be overcome by a strong education system: "That children from poor and illiterate homes tend to remain poor and illiterate is an unacceptable failure of our schools....They *can* break the cycle...."

Today there are programs that try to solve this problem. The Association of American Publishers and the International Reading Association have formed a program for *at-risk children*. At-risk children are often poor, homeless, or both, who run a higher risk of having social problems—like illiteracy or delinquency—than children from different backgrounds. The objective of this program is not only to provide instruction to these children, but also to offer literacy assistance to their parents or guardians—if necessary—at the same time. The project began in 1989 in Kansas City, Missouri, with 40 children ages five to 12. A program of this nature works to bring information and knowledge to both parent and child, thereby building self-esteem and worth in both.

Writer and editor Walter Anderson has made a career out of reading and writing, yet in his childhood he often found it difficult to bring a book into the house. In his book, *Read With Me*, he recalls a day when his father caught him reading:

> The kitchen door opened—and I was caught cold. It was too late to hide the evidence; the proof was there in my lap. My father, drunk, his face flushed, reeled before me, glowering, menacing. My legs started to tremble. I was nine years old. I knew I would be beaten. There could be no escape; my father had found me reading....
> "Doin' that crap again!" he shouted.
> I'm sor-" I tried to apologize, but the book, *Gulliver's Travels*, was slapped from my hands before I could finish my plea.
> "Then terrified, I made a second mistake: I

tried to stop the book from falling. When I reached for it, a hard, stinging punch to my shoulder knocked me from the chair.

....My father had been a victim of alcoholic, abusive parents when he was a boy, and he had attended only a few years of elementary school. Thus, when he was an adult, he could barely read, probably not as well as an average third-grader—an embarrassing handicap that I'm sure inspired much of the jealous rage he felt toward readers.

An alcoholic like his parents before him, my father had hit me before, many times and harder, and in the years that followed he would hit me again, many times and harder, until finally I quit high school at sixteen and left home. His persistent rage about my reading when I was a boy, though, frustrated me more than all other abuse; it made me feel squeezed in the jaws of a terrible vise, because I would not, I *could* not stop reading....My mother, who wrote notes and reports for my father and did much of his reading, understood. Although she was acutely aware of the danger, she nevertheless encouraged me to read, believing that through reading I would find my way. Thus I defied my father—and, as I've recalled here, sometimes I paid a price for that defiance.

It was worth it.

FOUR

TEACHING ADULTS TO READ

Teaching adults to read is different than teaching children. Because they have lived longer and experienced more than children, adults have more advanced reasoning and judgment skills. They are independent. Their life experience is much greater than that of the child who is first learning to read.

Many adults in illiteracy programs have jobs, children, and other "grown-up" concerns. Time is valuable to them, and they don't want a tutor who is condescending, inconsiderate, or critical. They need motivation. And they need confidence.

Unfortunately, too many adult literacy programs use teaching methods similar to those in traditional classrooms. These methods have failed the students once, and they often fail again. Students come to literacy programs of their own free will; no one can force them to stay. They attend classes only as long as they want. If they aren't interested and excited about learning, or if they feel they aren't making any progress, they'll quit.

Too often, adult learners give up. They drop out of programs before they reach one or all of their goals. Students may feel their needs are not being met by the tutor. Maybe the method of instruction isn't working. Maybe the student feels uncomfortable with the tutor or other members in a group program. They may have thought becoming literate would take a few months instead of the years it really takes. Sometimes feelings of failure and depression make them give up.

Teachers and administrators of literacy programs have discovered that a positive personal relationship between student and teacher can keep a student involved and satisfied with their progress. A teacher becomes a mentor, role model, and builder of self-esteem. When trust develops, students are much more likely to stay in literacy programs. If the student participates in a group program, a supportive, community feeling among the group keeps them from dropping out.

Statistics show that dropout rates increase with poverty, minority status, and the severity of the student's illiteracy. Sometimes learners have personal situations that make meeting their goals difficult. If a student moves, it can be hard to start all over again with a new tutor. Personal or family problems and ill health are other common reasons for students to drop out.

Perhaps a tutor can help his or her student locate medical help or family counseling. Maybe the student needs help finding child care in order to attend lessons, or needs assistance paying for independent reading materials. Whenever a tutor can help, it greatly increases the chance of the student reaching his or her goals.

Different Kinds Of Illiteracy

Statistics about illiteracy are difficult to sort through. We've said that 27 million people in this country are illiterate, but other sources quote much higher numbers like 45 million or even 72 million. Other sources say that only three or four million

A literacy tutor must be committed to his or her student. It can take a long time to learn to read, and a good teacher is willing to stick with the student.

adults can't read. How can there be a difference of almost 70 million people between these figures?

When people hear the word illiterate, many think only of people who can read nothing or very little, or who may not even know the alphabet. If we consider only those who are completely illiterate or are unable to read anything but the simplest of texts, then about 27 million adults, aged 17 and over, are illiterate in the United States today. They are below the level of functional literacy—at the third- or fourth-grade level. They cannot read street signs, phone books, or other items one must read to function in the workplace and in life.

But if a person is expected to be able to read newspapers or simple fashion magazines (about eighth-grade reading level), than 45 million people could be considered illiterate. Let's make the standards even higher. If individuals are expected to read at the high school level, which would mean reading and comprehending such magazines as *Time* or *Newsweek*, then 72 million people could be classified as illiterate. This is one-third of our nation.

It doesn't matter how we define illiteracy. We will never have an exact count of illiterates because so many of them hide their secret and pretend they can read "like everyone else." We don't need an exact figure to become concerned about education.

The Functionally Illiterate Stage

The functionally illiterate individual can read nothing, or only the simplest signs or instructions. Some of these people, less than half, are not native English speakers. These students often leave literacy programs speaking, but not reading or writing English. The larger portion of functional illiterates are English-speaking Americans who have attended school, maybe even graduated from high school, but never learned to read. Some of these individuals have a type of reading disability like dyslexia that has made it more difficult for them to learn. These individuals, like their younger counterparts, need special help when learning to read.

Totally illiterate individuals are often very afraid of failure. They have lived with embarrassment and shame all their lives. Courses developed for these people must take that into consideration.

Beginning readers often perform better in one-on-one instruction where they can develop a strong relationship with the teacher. At this stage of literacy, good teaching is often considered the most important factor of success. Programs also need to allow sufficient time for progress. Once the student understands that moving from no literacy to functional literacy may take years, he must be in a program that will stay with him throughout the entire process.

Adult students do not want to be treated like children, nor do they want reading materials written for children. Maybe you remember the primary readers you had in kindergarten and first grade. They said things in simple sentences like, See Jane. See Jane run. These books wouldn't interest you today; imagine how an adult would feel if this were all he or she were given to study. It would be embarrassing, and it would be hard to stay interested. Adults need special, high-interest materials that are geared toward more mature readers.

Many literacy programs are working to publish new texts for the beginning adult reader. For example, a group called Literacy Volunteers of New York City publishes beginning books designed to look like adult books. Other groups produce travel or food books that are less embarrassing for an adult to be seen with than a "Dick and Jane" reader.

The Functionally Literate Stage

Once a student has reached the fourth- or fifth-grade reading level, advancing further can be an even bigger challenge. To reach higher levels, the student must acquire general knowledge in order to

Characteristics Of A Successful Tutor

1. *A positive attitude.* An encouraging tutor can keep a student from giving up.

2. *Courtesy and thoughtfulness.* A tutor should start and stop a lesson on time. A tutor should never skip a lesson. A tutor should be willing to listen to a student's concerns and personal problems.

3. *Humor.* A lesson should be fun.

4. *Humility.* A tutor should be willing to admit a mistake. It will make the student feel there is a "team effort" in the class. A tutor should listen if a student says a method is not working for them.

5. *Patience.* Learning can be time consuming and frustrating. The tutor should never seem rushed or annoyed.

6. *Understanding.* A tutor must remember that adult learners are not children: They have the experience, knowledge, and information of an adult even if they have not had an adequate formal education.

7. *Flexibility.* If a tutor realizes one method works better for a student than another, he or she should be willing to change the lesson plan.

8. *Creativeness.* A tutor should look for lessons that are challenging and interesting. Materials should never be so difficult that they frustrate the reader, nor so easy that they insult him or her.

9. *Encouraging.* Tutors should make the student feel comfortable when participating in the lesson.

10. *Alert.* A tutor should be able to recognize problems that make learning especially difficult for a student, like poor eyesight, a family problem, or a learning disability.

comprehend and use what is read. Advanced reading demands more than just recognizing words. The reader must also be able to grasp subtle messages and have a strong background of information.

Let's imagine for a moment a creature from another planet arrives at your local book store. Somehow, the creature is able to read English, but it knows little about the history of planet Earth. He picks up a newspaper and reads the headline, "President To Cut Defense Budget." The creature doesn't know what the president is, much less the defense budget. Plus, it doesn't understand how the word "cut" is used in this sentence. It may be hard to believe that an adult in our society could have similar difficulties, but even literate people often know a lot less about their world than they think they know.

Literacy students must use reading to increase their knowledge of the world and acquire critical thinking skills. On the average, only about half the students at intermediate literacy levels progress on to the eighth-grade level because they are unable to combine reading skills with general knowledge.

Teachers have discovered a number of techniques that work with these students. They start with short reading selections, then gradually increase their length; increase the number of assignments that require writing; encourage students to form opinions about what they read; and use mature reading materials that might include history, civics, or science.

One program called Project: LEARN of Cleveland, Ohio, started a special discussion group for its intermediate students. Volunteer tutors in a Cleveland literacy program realized that adult beginning readers seldom had an opportunity to speak with anyone but their tutors about what they were reading. They believed that any encouragement the students could offer each other would be valuable, so they invited 12 of them, ages 25 to 60, to attend a discussion group.

Ten students came to the first meeting. They read a "hi-lo" book (high-interest, low vocabulary) that the tutors hoped would be interesting to everyone. Then they answered questions and were encouraged to offer their ideas and opinions about the story. The students encouraged each other, and all of them agreed that the meeting was helpful.

Today the Project: LEARN members help choose the books they discuss. Usually the topics relate to social or family issues; sometimes they read books about history. The students talk about topics such as why a character behaves the way he or she does, or how they might behave in a different situation. Sometimes they try to predict what will happen next. The discussion groups are always lively and informative. As one organizer noted, "The Project: LEARN Book Club is not a place to feel like a beginning reader. It is a place to feel like a functioning adult in a literate society."

Advanced Literacy

Studies show that among America's young adults, illiteracy is not a major problem—*literacy* is. What exactly does this mean? In 1985 the National Assessment of Educational Progress conducted a test of 3,500 young adults ages 21 to 25. While the majority of those tested could adequately perform reading

Many Americans can read the words in a newspaper, but they are unable to make sense of them because they do not have enough background information.

tasks that required low levels of literacy, sizable numbers were unable to do well on more difficult material. The more challenging the task, the fewer young adults who could complete it. Only 20 percent of those surveyed had advanced reading skills, and only about one-half were judged to be *adept* readers. In other words, although these individuals were not totally illiterate, they were not literate enough to perform well in our society.

Because literacy standards in the American workplace have risen, there are now programs designed to increase *vocational* or career literacy. These programs work to help students advance in their careers, improve work habits, and gain self-esteem. Some are offered by employers, while others are part of community outreach projects.

Other advanced literacy programs focus on raising the students' possession of knowledge. An educator named E.D. Hirsch, Jr., wrote a book in 1987 called *Cultural Literacy*. In this book, Hirsch notes that national literacy "at a very high level" was vital to the economic and democratic survival of the United States. To Hirsch, literacy is more than reading at the fourth- or eighth-grade level. The literate person must possess a large amount of information about history, the arts, people, places, and events.

It is definitely a good thing to know a lot about our world. But Hirsch forgets another characteristic of the highly literate person: the ability to *use* his or her knowledge. A culturally literate person uses what he or she knows to help understand the world and the self. It takes effort and desire to be a highly literate person. And it depends as much on what one learns outside of school as in. Literacy is a life-long challenge. It is enriched by personal interests and endeavors.

Being literate can mean a lot of things. It might mean reading just well enough to fill out a job application. Maybe it means reading well enough to understand simple newspaper articles that don't require much background knowledge. Perhaps it means understanding complex ideas, or having read great works of literature and comprehended them. The word literacy can be used in all of these contexts. But perhaps the true definition of a literate person is someone who, regardless of reading level, uses his or her literacy to learn new things about the world, the self, and others.

FIVE

WHAT'S BEING DONE?

Whether one claims there are 27 million, 45 million, or 72 million illiterates in this country, only about four million adults were involved in literacy programs in the late 1980s. One literacy specialist has determined that only two to four percent of the people who need help are receiving it. It can be difficult to reach illiterate adults and encourage them to join literacy programs. It also can be difficult for them to muster the courage it takes to admit their problem.

But if all American adults who need literacy training suddenly were to seek help, the existing programs would not have the funds, staff, or materials to teach them. Because statistics indicate that the number of individuals seeking help will increase each year, there must be continuing efforts to form new and successful literacy programs. As Liz Smith, journalist and a literacy advocate, put it, "We realize we can teach only a fraction of the more than a million New Yorkers who cannot read effectively. Truly, I think we'd be lucky to teach a thousand a year. Now what does that mean? It means a thousand people change their lives, become liberated, free."

Computer Learning

Although the use of computers for literacy training is still limited, many tutors are discovering that computers are helpful tools in the instruction process. Students can use computers to practice lessons over and over again. A computer also gives students

Working toward literacy can be frightening. It means admitting one has a problem and committing to years of study. But no one who learns to read ever regrets the work.

privacy and enables them to correct their own mistakes without feeling embarrassed. Some computer programs can also help the tutor determine a student's reading ability more accurately, and thus provide for more effective training.

Finding software for instruction can be difficult, however. Programs for totally illiterate individuals are scarce, although materials designed for older elementary school students can be used for slightly more advanced adult learners. Unfortunately, these programs, like the reading materials available for beginning readers, are often of little interest to the adult reader.

As time goes on, computers will become increasingly important and useful to literacy projects.

New software will be designed just for adult learners that will offer individualized training. Perhaps many people who are afraid to work one-on-one with a human tutor will benefit when computers play a greater role in adult literacy programs.

Volunteer Projects

Today many of the most successful literacy programs are those that use the skills of trained volunteers. Some experts worry that volunteers, who seldom receive more than 10 or 15 hours of training, don't have the education or skill necessary to teach adult illiterates. But the efforts of these unpaid men and women is very important to the ongoing campaign for American literacy.

Two of the most well-known volunteer programs are Laubach Literacy International (LLI) and Literacy Volunteers of America (LVA). Frank C. Laubach founded LLI in 1955. It sponsors literacy programs around the world (LLI serves the United States through Laubach Literacy Action).

Personalized teaching and phonics instruction (the sounding out of letters of the alphabet) provide the basis of the Laubach program. Laubach Literacy Action offers training through the efforts of some 98,000 volunteers, providing literacy training and English as a second language instruction to about 100,000 students on a one-to-one basis. There are 600 Laubach affiliates in 45 states.

Literacy Volunteers of America was founded by Ruth Colvin in the early 1960s. One day Colvin learned that in her home town of Syracuse, New York, there were more than 11,000 illiterate adults.

Reading to a child is just one of the pleasures that reading can bring.

"I was shocked," says Colvin. "I had never considered illiteracy to be a problem in America. Didn't
we guarantee public education?... My middle-class
life in the suburbs had screened me from a world
where books are not opened and newspaper head-
lines are not read."

When Colvin learned that nothing was being
done for these people, she decided to lead the effort.
After studying the Laubach method and working
with reading specialists from Syracuse University,
Colvin began creating a new teaching method. She
discovered that people learn in different ways. In
1969, Colvin and another woman, Dr. Jane Root, fin-
ished the innovative Literacy Volunteers training
materials, which covered a number of different
instruction techniques. Today, LVA has more than

80,000 participants in 39 states.

Laubach Literacy Action and Literacy Volunteers of America are the two largest volunteer efforts in the country, with chapters throughout the United States. But many state and local programs are working to help adult non-readers also. As many as 7,000 community-based literacy programs are in operation around the country.

Government Involvement

The government supports two large efforts to fight illiteracy: Adult Basic Education, which is the country's largest program, and the military's remedial training for its recruits. In addition, the Adult Education Act funds programs that benefit educationally disadvantaged adults. In 1990, $160 million was allocated for the Adult Education Act—about one percent of the Department of Education's budget.

Legislation to benefit the illiterate has increased in recent years. The Family Support Act of 1988, for example, authorized education and job training for welfare recipients. The Omnibus Trade and Competitiveness Act of 1988 authorized several new adult literacy education and training programs. The Stewart B. McKinney Homeless Assistance Act offers literacy and remedial education to homeless adults.

President George Bush and the nation's governors have set a goal: They want 100 percent literacy in the United States by the year 2000. To achieve this, two major bills were introduced to Congress in 1990. One bill, sponsored by Representative Tom Sawyer of Ohio, hopes to increase Adult Education Act funding from $160 million to $250 million a year. The House of

Representatives approved the bill overwhelmingly. The Senate sponsored a similar bill that passed unanimously, calling for an increase of $230 million to the Adult Education Act.

Both bills hope to bring more federal leadership to the problem of illiteracy. For example, a national center for literacy would be created to write national education goals, develop better teaching methods, and train instructors. The bills would also provide incentive for businesses in the United States to get involved with education programs. Representative Sawyer sponsored the House bill because he recognizes the problems illiteracy poses in the workplace. "If you can't read, write, and do basic math, you just cannot be a truly productive American. It's just that simple."

While the federal government is working to end illiteracy, critics believe that much more could—and should—be done. Some claim that the government is treating a serious problem with mild solutions. In the coming years, literacy advocates hope the federal government will do more than just offer money to a few nationally known literacy projects. They hope that America will look for more universal solutions—ones that will one day make illiteracy in the United States a thing of the past.

Problems

Volunteers across America are the reason that literacy projects are able to operate. Nonetheless, many literacy specialists believe that for programs to be effective, teachers need more training than many volunteer programs are able to offer.

There are not enough tutors or money to help all the illiterate people in the United States. Without both, it will be difficult to reach the goal of 100 percent literacy by the year 2000.

Teaching adults is not recognized as a profession different from traditional teaching, so few schools offer education to train teachers to work with adult non-readers. Literacy specialists hope that the future will see more paid professionals in the field of adult education and superior training for volunteers. College classes that focus specifically on adult education are needed for students who want to work for literacy programs.

Illiteracy projects never seem to have enough money. Although government and private donors help support these programs, there is never enough money to meet all expenses. Illiteracy programs must rent space to teach their students; they must pay staff members; and they must buy materials and instructional tools. With the increasing number of illiterates who seek help each year, literacy workers fear they will not be able to offer help to all who want it.

The Future

There are major advertising campaigns to combat illiteracy on national television. We've heard President and Mrs. Bush speak about the problem. We've learned about legislation passed by the government to help. Corporations and business leaders across the country are spending millions of dollars to help their employees learn to read or improve their skills. Thousands of volunteers around the country are doing what they can to teach adults to read, as are programs on the national and local levels. Yet there is still a high number of illiterates in our country, and no way to reach them all. The problem is larger than our resources. All these efforts combined probably serve less than 10 percent of the illiterate population.

As we work to solve the problem of adults who are already illiterate, we should keep one thing in mind: There are about 52 million citizens in the United States under the age of 14. Any one of these children may never learn to read, which means they'll join the millions of American adults who are already illiterate. If we are ever to see a decrease in illiteracy, we will have to make a firm commitment to *prevent* it, not just *cure* it. No student should leave the public school system without having learned to read.

GLOSSARY

AT-RISK CHILDREN. Children who, because of their social or economic background, run a higher risk of being illiterate, taking part in criminal activity, or participating in other anti-social behavior.

CULTURAL LITERACY. A phrase coined by author E.D. Hirsch, Jr., that means to possess a large amount of knowledge or information. Many believe that to be culturally literate, one must not only possess this information but must use it to better himself or his environment.

DYSLEXIA. A biological impairment that makes it difficult to read the printed word. The cause is unknown.

EMPOWERMENT. The achievement of independence, self-reliance, and power in the individual.

FUNCTIONALLY ILLITERATE. Reading at or below the fourth-grade level.

HIEROGLYPHICS. A system of writing used by the ancient Egyptians.

IDEOGRAPHS. Two or more pictographs (drawings) combined to make the written communication of an idea.

LINGUIST. Someone who studies language.

LOGOGRAPHS. A method of written communication that uses specific symbols or signs to represent spoken words and sounds.

PHONICS. A method of teaching beginners to read using the sounds of the alphabet.

PICTOGRAPHS. Drawings that represent an idea or a thing.

READING DISABILITIES. Biological problems that slow or completely prevent a student from learning. Dyslexia is a reading disability.

BIBLIOGRAPHY

Books

Anderson, Walter. *Read With Me*. Boston: Houghton Mifflin Company, 1990.

Hirsch Jr., E.D. *Cultural Literacy*. Boston: Houghton Mifflin Company, 1987.

Kozol, Jonathan. *Illiterate America*. New York: Doubleday, 1985.

Lane, Martha A., ed. "Handbook for Volunteer Reading Aides." Philadelphia: Lutheran Church Women, 1984.

Other Publications

Arnove, Robert F., and Harvey J. Graff. "National Literacy Campaigns: Historical and Comparative Lessons." *Phi Delta Kappan*. November 1987: 202.

Chall, Jeanne S., Elizabeth Heron, and Ann Hilferty. "Adult Literacy: New and Enduring Problems." *Phi Delta Kappan*. November, 1987: 191.

Collins, Catherine. "2 Measures Provide Ammunition in U.S. Campaign Against Illiteracy." *Los*

Angeles Times, August 26, 1990: D2.

Fineman, Marcia Pollack. "Project: LEARN—Adults
    Become Readers." *Library Journal*, March 1,
    1987: 45.

Irwin, Paul M., "Adult Literacy Issues, Programs, and
    Options." *CRS Issue Brief*. October 1, 1990.

Levine, Sarah L., and Sally Osbourne. "Living and
    Learning With Dyslexia." *Phi Delta Kappan*,
    April 1989: 594.

Lewis, Anne C. "Reading the Writing On the Wall."
    Phi Delta Kappan. March 1988: 468.

Pipho, Chris. "Sorting Out the Data On Adult
    Illiteracy." *Phi Delta Kappan*. May 1988: 630.

Prete, Barbara. "Literacy Matters: Business Defines Its
    Role." *Publisher's Weekly*. May 26, 1989: 20.

Schuster, Edgar. "The Pursuit of Cultural Literacy." *Phi
    Delta Kappan*, March, 1989: 539.

"Adult Literacy Issue: An Update." *Eric Digest*, Center
    on Education and Training For Employment,
    No. 89.

Volunteer Network News. U.S. Department of
    Education—Adult Education and Literacy.
    Winter, 1989.

INDEX

About The Author

Elizabeth Sirimarco graduated from the University of Colorado where she studied literature, art history, and film. She lives in Laguna Beach, California, with her two cats, Hal and Roger. She has begun a project to write books for the illiterate and students of English as a second language.

Photo Credits

AP/Wide World Photos   9, 19, 26
Literacy Volunteers of America, 12, 31, 38, 44, 50, 53, 55, 58